To John.

Best wishes

English Electric Traction Chester to Holyhead

Volume 2: 1984 to 2012

Contents

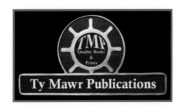

Ty Mawr Publications

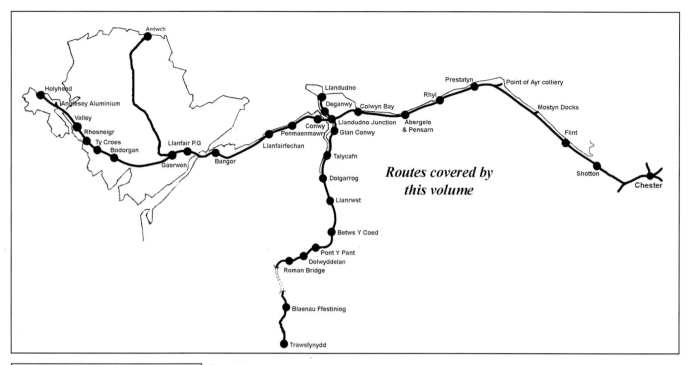

Routes covered by this volume

Published by

**Ty Mawr Publications
Holmes Chapel
Cheshire
UK
www.tymawrpublications.co.uk**

© 2012 Steve Morris

**ISBN
978-0-9552354-6-7**

Design & typesetting by
Steve Morris

Front cover
37407 heads 1K61 the 10.22 Bangor to Crewe through Dwygyfylchi near Penmaenmawr on July 22nd 1997. **Photo Steve Morris.**

Back cover top left
The summer dated 2D90 16.44 departure for Derby waits to depart Llandudno behind 20032-20007 on September 24th 1991. **Photo Pat Webb.**

Back cover top right
Filling in for the booked class 37/4, 37116 "Sister Dora" heads 1D81 the 18.18 Crewe to Bangor through Aber on June 8th 1996. **Photo Dave Trains.**

Back cover middle left
September 11th 1984 and 40013 passes the armless post of Llangwyllog up distant signal heading the morning Amlwch to Llandudno Junction service. On this particular day it was loaded to over 800 Tonnes and the journey down the branch on the damp rail proved to be particularly challenging for driver Mike Lunn. **Photo Peter Hanahoe.**

Back cover middle right
Headed by 57304, 50044 "Exeter" brings up the rear of 1Z51, a return charter to Euston having left North Llanrwst at 13.14. The location is just south of Glan Conwy. The class 50 would take over the rest of the working at Llandudno Junction. **Photo Dave Trains.**

Back cover bottom left
55019 "Royal Highland Fusilier" at Pentre Du near Aber heading for Holyhead on a DPS charter to Holyhead. May 13th 2000. **Photo Peter Hanahoe.**

Back cover bottom right
A one off for the class, 73002/006 seen on the outskirts of Rhyl heading for Llandudno Junction working "The Jolly JA's" charter. March 12th 1994. **Photo Garnedd Jones.**

Acknowledgements
In common with volume one of this series I am indebted to a number of people who have provided images and information used in this publication. In particular to Peter Hanahoe, Dave "Trains" Williams, Garnedd Jones, Ron Watson-Jones, Dave Rapson and Pat Webb for their invaluable assistance and last but not least to Sue, Matt and Jack for their patience throughout the production process.
I hope this publication serves as a reminder to the reader of the service provided by these British built products, an era that will never be repeated. Please feel free to drop me a line via the Ty Mawr Publications website with any comments, corrections or otherwise!

Steve Morris, Holmes Chapel, September 2012. www.tymawrpublications.co.uk

References
"The Allocation History of BR Diesels and Electrics" parts 1 to 5 by Roger Harris.
Class 37 loco group website www.c37lg.co.uk

INTRODUCTION

Welcome to the second in this series of publications looking back at English Electric built locomotives in operation between Chester and Holyhead. This volume covers the period between 1984 and the present day. It follows the same format as the first volume being split into several chapters, each dealing with a particular section of the line with the subject matter dealt with on a geographical basis rather than by date or locomotive class. Once again, only locomotive types built by English Electric are included, those fitted with English Electric power units and produced by other builders do not feature. As a result, classes 20, 37, 40, 50, 55 and 73 are covered. Once again, the main focus is to provide a pictorial review of the products produced by what was probably the most successful locomotive builder in the UK, operating in part of the country which was dominated by Diesels for over forty years.

A summary of how things progressed for each locomotive type follows below.

Up until the end of the period covered by volume 1 in 1983, class 20s had only made three appearances in the area, none of which were on regular timetabled workings. This remained the case until the early part of 1985 following the use of the class, from April the previous year, in the North West in general, particularly in the Warrington and Wigan areas. Possibly the first appearance for the class on a routine working involved the use of 20016/034 on a freight duty from Warrington to Llandudno Junction on March 1st 1985 prior to working back light to Wigan Springs Branch. Even more surprising was the appearance of 20092/139 on a Stafford to Llandudno and return passenger duty, see page 27, which took place on June 22nd 1985 during the Crewe station remodelling period. This was the first use of the class on a timetabled passenger duty across the North Wales Coast, the next such working and first passenger duty for the class as far as Holyhead not taking place until October 26th 1988 with 20158/139 towing failed 47611 on 1D33 the 07.55 Coventry to Holyhead, see page 59. Appearances of this nature would take place several times until the early 1990s. In terms of diagrammed passenger duties, class 20s were utilised for several summer dated workings from the Derby and Stoke areas to Llandudno between 1989 to 1991 with 20202/199 even making it as far as Blaenau Ffestiniog on a fill in turn on September 26th 1989. The final such working actually took place as late as August 22nd 1992 with 20090/132 being provided for 1D21, the 07.30 Nottingham to Llandudno and 11.40 return.
More regular appearances on freight duties commenced during the summer of 1985 with 20049/056 visiting Penmaenmawr for a ballast working on July 22nd, the first of many such appearances for the class. 20023 and later 20157 were based at Chester depot from August 1985 for driver training in preparation for taking over Point of Ayr colliery MGR workings. 200160/060 headed the 21.00 Point of Ayr to Fiddlers Ferry service on August 22nd 1985. However, it would be two years before the class saw regular use on these diagrams, an early example being the use of 20056/071 on August 21st 1987.

The first appearance of the class past Bangor (20153/165 having got that far in 1979, see volume 1) took place on January 3rd 1986 when 20183/214 headed a 9X11 16.11 Crewe Gresty Road to Gaerwen engineers train. This was followed almost 12 months later with 20005/135 getting all the way through to Holyhead at the head of a special Freightliner on December 5th. Class 20s continued to appear on freight duties up to the early 1990s, the most regular being Point of Ayr MGR and Penmaenmawr ballast duties with a number of Freightliners to Holyhead and an occasional trip working from Chester thrown in for good measure. The 1990s also saw the class utilised on Hunslet Barclay operated weed killer services in North Wales as far as Trawsfynydd and Amlwch. The final chapter for the class commenced early in 1999 when DRS commenced their use on Nuclear flask traffic to and from Valley, something that continues to the present day, over fifty years since the first appearance of the class in North Wales!

Above The first recorded class 20 hauled ballast working from Penmaenmawr took place on July 22nd 1985. Here, 20049/056 are seen with their train being loaded at the quarry sidings prior to working to St Helens. They would return the following day on the same service along with 20001/016 on a similar duty.
Photo Ron Watson-Jones.

In common with class 20s, class 37s had only made a small number of appearances between Chester and Holyhead up until 1984. However, this was soon to change and within a short time they became regular visitors to the area. Early workings involved running-in turns from Crewe works, particularly for refurbished examples of the class. 37401 appeared on June 19th 1985 working to Llandudno on a rake of redundant coaching stock. However, by October of this year an alternative running-in method involved double heading a Cardiff to Bangor or Holyhead and return service from Crewe with the diagrammed class 33 or 47, something which lasted until May 1987. Workings to and from Llandudno using redundant stock continued for several more years. 37719, the final class 37 to be refurbished making the trip on the 19th of March 1989.

Of interest, during this period 37073 made no less than eight test runs between November 1987 and January 1988, there were clearly a number of problems to rectify in this particular case! The final test run working is thought to have taken place during March 1992 with sister locomotive 37074 being noted on the 19th of that month on 1D05 the 12.35 Crewe to Llandudno Junction and return.

Above June 19th 1985 and newly refurbished 37401, ex 37268, is seen at Greenfield heading back to Crewe from Llandudno on what is thought to be one of the first running-in turns for the class in North Wales. Following a period based in Scotland to work the far North lines, this particular example would find itself based at Crewe in the late 1990s working regularly between Crewe and Holyhead. In later years it would work the final class 37 hauled freight service out of the Anglesey Aluminium plant near Holyhead in multiple with 37425, this being as late as October 31st 2009, see page 50. **Photo Dave Sallery.**

Spasmodic appearances on non running-in turn passenger duties commenced in 1988. What is thought to be the first passenger turn to Holyhead took place on March 4th of that year when 37427 worked a 1Z16 20.50 rugby special from Cardiff to the port before returning ECS. More regular passenger duties in North Wales commenced in December 1988 with the introduction of a Cardiff to Rhyl diagram for a class 37/4 following the withdrawal of the Canton based class 155 Sprinter fleet due to door problems. 37426 headed the first such working on December 16th, the final one being behind 37431 on March 15th 1989. Several Euston workings were entrusted to the class in 1990, the most notable being the appearance of 37045 working a rake of air conditioned stock in lieu of a failed class 47 between Crewe and Holyhead and return on Sunday September 23rd 1990, see page 55. 1993 saw the start of a period of almost eight years where the class reigned supreme in terms of passenger workings in North Wales. This followed the introduction of a number of loco hauled diagrams covering routes between Holyhead and Crewe, Manchester, Birmingham and even Blackpool which were entrusted to a newly created pool of class 37/4s based at Crewe. It is these workings for which class 37s will be best remembered for in North Wales, bringing a welcome change to the tide of Sprinter operated services that had all but killed off loco hauled secondary passenger services in the UK. The first such working took place behind 37429 on May 17th 1993, the very last one being headed by the same locomotive on January 20th 2001. Apart from the occasional charter train that was it as far as North Wales passenger duties for the class were concerned.

The first regular freight diagram for the class in the area was a Fridays Only duty from Peak Forest to Penmaenmawr for loading with roadstone for Manchester Hope Street. This commenced on March 20th 1987 behind 37129/209, see page 44, although refurbished 37s would become the norm for this duty until being taken over by class 60s in 1992. Occasional use on a number of container train workings to Holyhead took place between 1987 and 1991 as well as the odd engineers duty. An interesting short term duty involved the use of the class on an Allied Steel and Wire scrap service from Anglesey Aluminium to Cardiff during March and April 1992 which also involved the use of class 37/9s. Other regular freight duties during the 1990s involved Petroleum Coke workings from Immingham to Anglesey Aluminium, fuel oil between Stanlow refinery and Holyhead, ballast from Penmaenmawr, chemicals to Mostyn docks, coal to Glan Conwy yard and the "Valley flasks" under EWS and DRS. Another regular freight duty for the class in the area took place between April 2007 and October 2009 on a weekly working from the RTZ Anglesey Aluminium plant conveying Aluminium billets for export. Finally, as with the class 20s, over fifty years since first being introduced to service this well respected member of the English Electric stable still sees use with DRS on nuclear flask workings to and from Valley as well as seasonal railhead treatment duties to Holyhead and track measurement test trains.

In contrast to volume 1 of this series, class 40s play a relatively minor role in this publication. The end of regular operation for the class came on January 22nd 1985, although the remaining members of the class had continued to appear on the route between Chester and Holyhead right up until the end. The final duty fell to 40143 which worked the 3A19 Bangor to Northampton parcels as far as Crewe on January 21st. Withdrawal for 40143, along with almost all of the other members of the class came the day afterwards. However, a number of workings by four examples retained for engineers trains continued for two years. In addition, 40122 which was reinstated for use on charter trains etc also made a number of visits on both passenger and freight turns until early 1988. A notable working took place on February 9th of that year when it worked from Crewe to Holyhead and back at the head of a London service, the last time a class 40 would do so, having taken over these duties almost 28 years earlier. April 2nd 1988 saw 40122 work "The Tubular Belle" railtour to Blaenau Ffestiniog and Holyhead. At the time it was though that this would draw a line under class 40 use in any form in North Wales. However, thanks to hard work by The Class Forty Preservation Society this proved not to be the case, as will be seen later.

Whilst class 50s had featured relatively often in North Wales during the 1970s, their use from 1976 onward was confined to charter trains. There was in fact a gap of almost eight years between 50046 working a scheduled service to Holyhead in June 1976 (see volume 1) up to March 1984 when 50018 was booked to work a charter to Blaenau Ffestiniog on the 10th of that month. Only a handful of appearances would follow between then and the present day, the most recent being that of 50044 during September 2011, see pages 32 and 96.

Last but not least, who would have thought it but "Deltics" have made five appearances and a pair of class 73s, although not actually Vulcan Foundry produced examples, one visit to the area to date, helped of course in part by the lifting of the ban on the use of preserved diesels on the mainline.

1.
Chester to Rhyl

In common with the format followed in volume one, at the beginning of each chapter in this publication we will take a look at the route as it was during the period which it covers. Apologies for any duplication in text between the two volumes that my occur as a result of this.

On leaving Chester station the line passes a depot on the right, home to several class 40's between duties up to late 1986, latterly the 97xxx variety. 20023 and 20157 were based here during the second half of 1985 for driver training and the odd class 20 and 37 would visit for servicing during the period covered by this publication. A major rebuild of this facility took place in the year 2000 prior to being used by Alstom to service a new fleet of class 175 DMU's which would of course spell the end for class 37 hauled passenger duties in North Wales at the start of 2001. The junction for Birkenhead, also on the right is next, before the line runs through tunnels and crosses Roodee Viaduct over the river Dee. This is followed by Saltney Junction, the line to Wrexham and Shrewsbury branching off to the left. The route continues onwards through Shotton without any major gradients to tackle, the British Steel/Corus complex visible across the river Dee. Next comes Connah's Quay, home to the Crumps' wagon works, which would see closure in the late 1990's, before reaching Flint. A few miles on is the Courtaulds factory at Greenfield, latterly served by a small number of fuel oil services until 1985. Holywell Junction comes next, then Mostyn, home to a dock complex on the river Dee. Class 37 hauled chemical trains ran to here during the 1990's serving the Warwick International Chemicals sidings as 6M62 17:52 SuO/20:05 TThO Saltend to Mostyn via Hooton and Ellesmere Port and a 09:15 MWFO Mostyn to Saltend return. The first such working took place behind Tinsley based 37244 on July 10th 1991. Point of Ayr colliery is the last industrial site on the Chester to Rhyl section. Class 20's would feature strongly here on MGR workings between 1987 and 1991 with an occasional working taking place as late as 1993, 20057/154 being noted heading to Fiddlers Ferry power station on February 2nd of that year. The line then heads along the coast through Prestatyn before running between the sea and numerous caravan parks to Rhyl.

Above
55019 "Royal Highland Fusilier" was the first Deltic to visit North Wales. This followed the failure of 50017 at Crewe whilst working 1Z55, a charter from London Euston to Holyhead that was run in conjunction with Coventry City football club. Here they can be seen passing Shotton en route Holyhead on October 8th 1999. The Deltic would later head the return service to Euston before working the stock ECS back to Crewe. **Photo Dave Rapson.**

Above
37414 waits departure from Chester whilst heading a Bangor to Crewe service on July 25th 1996.
Photo Steve Morris.

Below
A complete contrast in weather conditions finds 37405 at the same location working 1K57 the 07.39 Holyhead to Crewe on February 6th 1996. **Photo Dave Trains.**

Right
Recently refurbished 37800, ex 37143 is seen at Chester on 1D45, the 08.47 Basford Hall to Llandudno running-in turn which utilised a rake of redundant coaches. August 15th 1986.
This was one of five trips along "the coast" before the all clear was given for 37800's release to Canton depot.
Photo Darran Moss.

Below
April 23rd 1986 and another trial run. This time 37501, ex 37005, pilots 33013 into Chester on 1V06 the 14.17 Bangor to Cardiff having worked to Bangor on 1D27 the 11.15 from Crewe earlier that day.
Photo Peter Hanahoe.

Below
37688 leads 37676 across Roodee Viaduct Chester heading 6D04, the Fridays only Hope Street to Penmaenmawr rake of empty RMC bogie wagons for loading with roadstone. The date is July 22nd 1988 and the return would be as 6J19 later that afternoon. Class 37s dominated this working until being replaced by class 60s in May 1992 although the flow only then lasted until the following year.
Interestingly the very first working of this nature involved the use of 40194 and 40035 on September 24th 1982 hauling a rake of PGA wagons. It would take until March 1987 before the regular flow commenced, 37209/129 being the locomotives involved, see page 44.
Photo Peter Hanahoe.

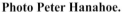

Above
20006 and 20141 pass through Roodee cutting Chester at the head of a Fiddlers Ferry to Point of Ayr MGR for loading on August 12th 1988. Class 20s dominated these workings between late 1987 and 1991. **Photo Peter Hanahoe.**

Below
Looking very smart in Royal Scotsman livery, 37428 passes Roodee Junction heading 1G79, the 18.22 Holyhead to Birmingham New Street on June 27th 2000.
Photo Dave Rapson.

Above
September 2nd 1984 and by now the use of class 40s on passenger turns was getting rare. However, on this day 40135 was provided for 1Z28, a charter from Holyhead to Carlisle, seen here at Shotton. **Photo Dave Rapson.**

Below
Just prior to the use of class 66s, a fine view of 37430 and 37412 at Shotton working 6C10, the 10.09 Penmaenmawr to Carnforth stone on April 23rd 1999. EWS would loose this business to Freightliner in June 2001. **Photo Dave Rapson.**

Above
At over 2000 Tonnes the Penmaenmawr to Hope Street roadstone flow was one of the heaviest regular freight working in North Wales. In this view, 37682 and 37679 are seen storming through Flint on the Fridays only afternoon service on June 24th 1988. **Photo Peter Hanahoe.**

Below
Bagillt and 55016 "Gordon Highlander" heads for Holyhead on a charter service from Milton Keynes on September 7th 2002. Painted in Porterbrook purple livery at the time, in recent years a more traditional coat of two tone green has been applied. **Photo Dave Rapson.**

Right
A few months before the end of regular class 20 hauled Point of Ayr MGR workings, 20143 and 20214 are seen passing Bagillt on a Fiddlers Ferry bound service on August 11th 1991. One of the last deep mines in Wales, Point of Ayr colliery closed in August 1996. 20143 succumbed to the cutters torch in August 1993 but 20214 lives on in preservation at the Lakeside & Haverthwaite Railway.
Photo Pat Webb.

Above
Following the withdrawal of the Canton based class 155 fleet in December 1988 due to door problems, a Cardiff to Rhyl and return service was introduced. Worked by a Canton class 37/4, this brought diagrammed class 37 hauled passenger services to North Wales for the first time. Departing Cardiff as 1M75 at 15.00 it returned as 1V19 at 19.06. In this view taken on May 9th 1989, 37426 is seen at Bagillt heading for Rhyl. The final such working would take place four days later behind 37431.
Photo Peter Hanahoe.

Right
40099 works the 7T89 Point of Ayr/Mostyn Trip through Bagillt back towards Chester. The date is July 25th 1984, withdrawal would come within three months and cutting at Doncaster works the following May.
Photo Dave Rapson.

Above
Running-in turns for non refurbished class 37s were rare. In this view, Thornaby based 37013 is seen heading from Llandudno back to Crewe on the rake of redundant coaches used as a suitable trailing load. **Photo Peter Hanahoe.**

Below
One of four class 40s reinstated in 1985, originally to assist in the Crewe station remodelling scheme, 97406 (ex 40135) passes Holywell Junction on a Penmaenmawr to Crewe ballast working on February 25th 1986. **Photo Peter Hanahoe.**

Above
The Trainload Coal freight sector organised a "motive power day" in North Wales on August 11th 1991. One of the trains concerned was headed by 20151 and 20059 and in this view they are seen passing Holywell Junction on the 14.45 Llandudno to Crewe.
Photo Peter Hanahoe.

Below
Not an uncommon occurrence. 47844 has just expired at Holywell Junction whilst heading 1A46, the 09.19 Holyhead to Euston on January 11th 2000. Toton based 37055 has just come to the rescue. Note the "Duke of Lancaster" ship moored on the coast in the background.
Photo Dave Rapson.

Above
Green liveried celebrity pair 20030 and 20064 head away from Mostyn on an afternoon Penmaenmawr to St Helens ballast working on May 31st 1990. Whilst based at Tinsley they had been unofficially named River Rother and River Sheaf for a period during 1987. Both were withdrawn from service within a few months of the above working. **Photo Dave Trains.**

Below
August 9th 1984. 40143 is seen passing Mostyn Dock at the head of 6E36, the Holyhead RTZ to Immingham empty coke working. 40143 would be the last of the class to work a train in North Wales prior to mass withdrawal of the fleet, this duty being the morning 3A19 Bangor to Northampton parcels on January 21st 1985. **Photo Peter Hanahoe.**

Right
Having worked to Holyhead earlier in the day, DRS's 20301 and 20302 are seen near Mostyn returning to Crewe on a 5K06 11.39 departure from Holyhead during a trial run prior to working a Royal train to Aberystwyth the following week. The date is May 30th 1996 and it would be several years before the class would be seen regularly in the area heading nuclear flask trains for DRS. **Photo Dave Rapson.**

Bottom
37425 waits to depart Mostyn docks on the 6E39 09.15 Mondays only chemical flow to Hull Saltend. It is January 18th 1993 and within four months this example would become one of the eight initial members of the class allocated to Crewe to work the new loco hauled duties in North Wales. **Photo T Driver.**

Left
July 30th 1985 at Mostyn sees 20194 and 20196 on a Penmaenmawr to St Helens ballast. There are 3 rows of hoppers for the sulphur traffic to Amlwch in the sidings. When the sulphur was carried in these, the loads were sheeted over. Just visible above the last wagon of the ballast train is one of the vans used for carrying the tarpaulins back to Mostyn ready for the next trip.
Class 20s had only started to appear on workings from Penmaenmawr the week before this image was recorded, see page 40.
Photo Peter Hanahoe.

Above
Regional Railways liveried 37414 leads 37426 in EWS colours past the previous entrance to Point of Ayr colliery at Talacre working 1D77, the 16.21 Birmingham New Street to Holyhead. August 20th 1999.
Photo Dave Rapson.

Below
A rare view of a single class 37 heading the Fridays only Hope Street to Penmaenmawr empties. The date is September 9th 1988 and 37676 is the locomotive concerned, seen here passing Llanerch-y-Mor near Mostyn. The other booked loco had failed at Holywell Junction. **Photo Peter Hanahoe.**

Left
A very early class 37 hauled freight working in North Wales occurred on June 5th 1987 when Tinsley based 37029 was provided for a Penmaenmawr to St Helens ballast duty. In this view the locomotive concerned is seen at Prestatyn.
Following use with DRS, 37029 can now be found in private ownership at North Weald on the Epping Ongar Railway.
Photo John Powell.

Right
Unreliability of the Crewe based 37/4s diagrammed for North Wales services often resulted in them being substituted by other members of the class. In this view, 37057 has been turned out for a second day on July 26th 2000 and is seen at Prestatyn heading 1K61, the 09.50 Holyhead to Crewe.
Photo Steve Morris.

Below
30th September 1984 and 40194 waits to enter the worksite at the head of a ballast train during track renewal at Prestatyn. This particular example would remain in traffic right to the end of regular use for the class. Withdrawal came on January 22nd 1985 and was followed by a quick move with 40192 to Doncaster works where they were quickly cut up.
Photo Peter Hanahoe.

Above
Having commenced use on DRS operated nuclear flask trains in North Wales in a few months earlier, 20312 and 20313 are seen near Prestatyn heading 7P41, the 11.30 Wednesdays only Valley to Sellafield on April 7th 1999.
Photo T Driver.

Below
An early class 37 running-in turn along the North Wales Coast involved refurbished 37404 (ex 37286) heading to Llandudno and back on the Crewe works test train on June 27th 1985. In this view the return working is seen passing through Rhyl. **Photo John Powell.**

2.
Rhyl to Llandudno Junction

Up to the early 1970s Rhyl had been one of North Wales' most popular resorts and particularly busy during summer months. However, by the 1980s road had overtaken rail as the main choice of transport for the large volume of holidaymakers that still frequented the area, with a reduction in passenger rail traffic to match. Leaving Rhyl the line runs alongside Marine Lake and its miniature railway to the right before crossing the River Clwyd. Holiday parks line the route onwards through Abergele and Pensarn before the first real climb since Chester, up the 1 in 100 gradient to Llandulas and on up to the summit located at the entrance to the 485 yard long Penmaenrhos tunnel. After emerging from the tunnel there is a downhill run along the coast with superb views out towards Llandudno before reaching the popular resort of Colwyn Bay. Within a few miles the line to Blaenau Ffestiniog and Trawsfynydd branches off to the left just before reaching Llandudno Junction. Glan Conwy yard, built following the closure of Colwyn Bay yard at the end of 1981 can be found adjacent to the branch. Llandudno Junction itself still had a depot, marshalling yard and a carriage servicing facilities, a regular haunt for English Electric class 37 and 40s during the early part of the period covered by this volume. However by the late 1990's these facilities had all but disappeared as a result of the run down of freight in North Wales.

Above
One of the original eight class 37/4s allocated to the Crewe based RCMC pool set up in May 1993 to cover the new locomotive hauled North Wales coast services was 37418. New to Cardiff Canton in June 1965 as D6971, this example was renumbered 37271 in 1974 and remained allocated to either Canton or Landore until refurbishment and transfer to Eastfield as 37418 in 1985. A period of almost five years working off Inverness followed until transfer to the Immingham Railfreight Petroleum pool in September 1990 prior to the move to Crewe mentioned above. Named "East Lancashire Railway" on April 22nd 1994, further moves to Toton in July 1999 and then Motherwell took place before heading back to its original depot, Cardiff Canton, in September 2001 primarily for use on Rhymney Valley passenger services. A final allocation to Motherwell took place in February 2003 where "418" spent much of its time working Scottish sleeper services until withdrawal on September 20th 2007. Fortunately this particular example was then preserved and moved to the East Lancashire Railway in March 2009 where, following a period of regular use it is currently under repair as a result of low oil pressure problems.
In the above image, 37418 is seen about to depart Rhyl on July 25th 1996 whilst working a morning Crewe to Bangor service midway through its period of six years or so spent in North Wales.
Photo Steve Morris.

Above
Bank holiday Monday August 28th 1989 and an additional service running as 1T06, an 08.15 departure from Blyth Bridge to Llandudno is seen leaving Rhyl behind 20071 and 20182. Following a day on the beach the return would be as 1T07 at 18.10, see page 29.
Photo Peter Hanahoe.

Below
37425 enters Rhyl station past the former Rhyl No. 2 signal box at the head of a Bangor to Crewe working on July 25th 1996. Closed in March 1990, this former LNWR type 4 box was built in 1900 and is grade II listed. Exactly what the future holds for it remains to be seen.
Photo Steve Morris.

Above
Following two class 50 hauled tours during 1984, it would be a further eight years before the class returned to the area. This involved the use of 50033 and 50050 on "The Festive 50's" railtour from London Euston to Blaenau Ffestiniog and Holyhead, the first double headed class 50 to North Wales, other than possibly on running-in turns from Crewe works during the 1970's. In this view the train passes Abergele signal box on the down working on December 5th 1992.
Photo Peter Hanahoe.

Above
37706 is seen recessed at Abergele station whilst working 6E36, the 15.50 Sundays only Holyhead RTZ to Immingham coke empties. The date is March 31st 1996 during a period of over seven years when members of the class were diagrammed for this duty.
Photo Dave Trains.

Right
For several years between 1985 and 1987, the four "departmental" class 40s were regular visitors to North Wales. Here, on June 16th 1986, 97806 (40135) heads towards Abergele on a Penmaenmawr to Crewe ballast working.
Photo Peter Hanahoe.

Above

June 4th 1998. 37415 runs alongside one of the numerous caravan parks in the area towards Abergele heading 1G97, the 10.48 Holyhead to Birmingham New Street. Following a lengthy period in store after withdrawal in 2003, this particular example is currently located at Long Marston awaiting possible re use on the Dartmoor Railway.
Photo T Driver.

Below

Llandulas and 37422 heads for Bangor on 1D65, the 10.24 departure from Crewe on a wintery December 29th 1995. 37422 was a regular performer in North Wales from May 1993 until May 1999. Named "Cardiff Canton" following a light overhaul at that depot in February 2003, 37422 would return to North Wales on several freight workings between 2006 and 2008.
Photo Dave Trains.

Above
English Electric built 43 class 73 Electro Diesel locomotives at its Vulcan Foundry works between 1965 and 1967. The only visit to North Wales for the class came when two of an original batch of 6 built at Eastleigh works in 1962 worked "The Jolly JA's" tour between Chester and Llandudno Junction on March 12th 1994. Here, Birkenhead North depot shunters 73006 and 73002 approach Llandulas on this working. **Photo Dave Trains.**

Below
37421 bursts out of Penmaenrhos tunnel near Colwyn Bay at the head of the 10.48 Holyhead to Birmingham New Street on May 2nd 2000. Following over seven years use in North Wales a further period of passenger duties in South Wales and then Scotland followed before withdrawal in September 2007. Preservation on the Pontypool and Blaenavon railway followed in 2009. **Photo T Driver.**

Above
A classic North Wales Coast view. 20151 and 20059 are seen on the approach Penmaenrhos tunnel on August 11th 1991. Colwyn Bay pier and promenade can be seen in the background.
20151 would only see a further five months service whilst 20059 entered preservation and is currently located at the Severn Valley Railway.
Photo Darran Moss.

Left
Bescot based 37201 "Saint Margaret" passes through Colwyn Bay station on a Penmaenmawr to Warrington Arpley ballast service during July 1996. Withdrawal for this example would come within a few weeks of this image being recorded. However, it would take until March 2009 for final disposal to take place following a number of years owned by Harry Needle Rail Ltd as a source of spares at Barrow Hill.
Photo Steve Morris.

Above
40195 heads a rake of ex LNER billet wagons carrying welded rail for Llandudno Junction through the outskirts of Colwyn Bay on May 16th 1984. It is running on new track, this section having been moved to allow construction of the new A55 "Expressway". **Photo Peter Hanahoe.**

Below
April 3rd 1990 and 37677 leads 37685 on 6D04, Manchester Ashburys to Penmaenmawr ARC stone empties towards Llandudno Junction. This was a relatively short lived flow and involved the use of converted 45T tank wagons owned by Tiger Leasing. **Photo Peter Hanahoe.**

Left
March 10th 1984. 40122 heads the "Conway Crusader" railtour into Llandudno Junction. Originating at Coventry, this visited Llandudno and Blaenau Ffestiniog and also involved the use of 40029 and 40047 plus 50018 which became the first of its type to visit Blaenau Ffestiniog and the first class 50 to North Wales in almost eight years, see page 33.
Photo Garnedd Jones.

Below
55016 "Gordon Highlander" is seen passing through Llandudno Junction station at the head of a Milton Keynes to Holyhead charter. 47635 had worked the service as far as Crewe before the Deltic took it to Holyhead and back to Milton Keynes. At the time of writing this was the last visit of a Deltic to North Wales. September 7th 2002.
Photo Larry Davies.

Left
Fifty Fund owned 50031 "Hood" and 50049 "Defiance" approach Llandudno Junction during a light engine test run from Crewe being conducted to test recently fitted TPWS equipment. 50049 would continue to Llandudno and Bangor before the pair were reunited and towed a failed 47750 from Llandudno Junction to Warrington prior to returning to Crewe later in the day. On November 1st 1997, 50031 became the first preserved class 50 to return to the mainline when it worked the Pilgrim Hoover railtour between Birmingham and Plymouth. At the time of writing this was the first and last visit for either of these locomotives to North Wales since the 1970s.
Photo Dave Trains.

Above
Arguably the most remarkable passenger working in North Wales took place on June 22nd 1985 when Tinsley duo 20139 and 20092 were turned out to work 1D04, the 05.34 Stafford to Llandudno and 1A66 return to Euston as far as Stafford during the Crewe station remodelling period. Other than a charter duty to Blaenau Ffestiniog in July 1979, this was the first class 20 passenger working in North Wales, and on a rake of air conditioned coaches at that! **Photo Ron Watson-Jones.**

Below
40135 waits to depart Llandudno Junction yard for Warrington Arpley on November 28th 1984. Withdrawn on January 22nd 1985, the final day of regular service for the class, 40135 was reinstated as 97406 in May of the same year and worked in departmental traffic until December 1986. It was eventually preserved by The Class Forty Preservation Society in early 1989 and is currently based at the East Lancashire Railway Bury. **Photo Dave Rapson.**

Rhyl to Llandudno Junction

Above
Opened in 1981 as a replacement for Colwyn Bay yard, Glan Conwy goods yard on the outskirts of Llandudno Junction dealt with a variety of local traffic until the late 1990's. In this view, 37675 is seen performing a shunt on May 17th 1994.
Photo Dave Trains.

Right
The first visit by 55016 to North Wales came during a light engine trial run with the Ian Riley Engineering owned 37197. Running as 0Z55, an 11.58 Crewe to Llandudno Junction and 0Z16 15.07 return, the pair are seen here waiting to return to Crewe on March 21st 2002.
Photo Mark Lloyd Davies.

Left
October 5th 1995 and 37517 is seen leaving Llandudno Junction working 6Z11, the 09.20 Thursdays only Glan Conwy yard to Milford West sidings. It is returning a rake of empty HEA hoppers that had earlier transported household coal to the freight depot.
This occasional working continued until June 1999 and was the last regular flow to use Glan Conwy. There have been recent rumours concerning the use of this yard to load containers of household waste onto trains for movement out of North Wales, although nothing has come of this to date.
Photo Dave Trains.

3.
Llandudno to Trawsfynydd

In common with Rhyl, Llandudno saw a huge reduction in rail passenger traffic from the late 1970s onwards. However, a number of summer dated services from the Stoke and Derby areas during a three year period between 1989 and 1991 brought the first passenger hauled services diagrammed for class 20s in North Wales to Llandudno. A return service to Blaenau Ffestiniog even took place during a fill in turn in behind 20202/199 on September 26th 1989, a duty which had been booked for a class 31, the first class 20 hauled timetabled passenger service to Blaenau. Class 40s were represented in the area by 40122 right up to 1986 with several appearances on a summer dated Stoke/Llandudno/Blaenau Ffestiniog diagram. Other visits by a class 40 continue, this time preserved 40145, the only to date being in June 2005 on "The Whistling Slater" tour, see page 32. The Branch to Blaenau Ffestiniog and Trawsfyndd covers some of the most scenic landscape in the country including the two mile 338 yard tunnel on the approach to Blaenau itself. The construction of Trawsfynydd nuclear power station in the late 1950s resulted in the opening of a connection with the Great Western line to Bala at Blaenau Ffestiniog in 1964 to permit the transport of nuclear flasks along the section. Class 40s covered these services as part of Trip 47 from Llandudno Junction during 1984 having taken over this duty in May 1982, see volume 1. The use of other English Electric traction on Conwy Valley flask workings was rare but not unknown, see pages 33 and 35. Having been the first Diesel locomotive type to work through to Blaenau Ffestiniog in February 1961, see volume 1, class 20s made occasional appearances on weed-killer duties from late 1989, an early example being 20902/906 on the 21st of September which made it right through to Trawsfynydd. Finally, the first appearance of a class 37 on the Bleanau Ffestiniog branch occurred on May 3rd 1993 with 37422 working a special service from Crewe prior to being named "Robert F Fairlie" at Bleanau, see page 34.

Above
20182 leads 20071 past Deganwy up distant signal at the head of 1T07, an 18.10 Llandudno to Blyth Bridge Bank Holiday special on August 28th 1989. This was one of a number of additional services provided during the annual "Potter's holidays" and was during the first year of summer dated class 20 passenger workings to Llandudno. The first took place on June 26th with 20090 and 20120 heading over from Blyth Bridge on the 1T06 down working, an 08.15 departure. The final appearance on a Llandudno turn involved 20090 (again) and 20132 working the 07.30 Saturdays only from Nottingham and 11.40 return on August 22nd 1992 following the failure of the booked class 47. **Photo Peter Hanahoe.**

Llandudno to Trawsfynydd

Above
On several occasions during the summer of 1985 and 1986 40122 worked a diagram between Stoke, Llandudno and Blaenau Ffestiniog and return. On one such occasion, 2D18, the 16.05 Blaenau Ffestiniog to Llandudno is seen entering the town ready to form the final leg, 1K38 the 18.15 back to Stoke on August 4th 1986. **Photo Ron Watson-Jones.**

Below
June 15th 2000 and Chester driver Dave Plumb is seen with 37415 working 1D45, the 17.19 Manchester Piccadilly to Llandudno catching the evening sun at Deganwy. A late entrant to North Wales duties, 37415 worked the last but one 37/4 service out of Holyhead as late as January 19th 2001. **Photo Peter Hanahoe.**

Above
A shortage of rolling stock led to a dead three car DMU comprising 53073, 59598 and 53865 being towed by 20208 and 20005 as the 2D59 08.15 Derby to Llandudno and 2P86 12.47 return on July 15th 1989. Here they are seen passing Deganwy station on the return journey.
Photo Peter Hanahoe.

Below
Recently refurbished 37684 (ex 37134) passes through Deganwy heading back to Crewe on 1K08, the 14.25 return test train from Llandudno. The date is March 20th 1987 and within a few weeks it was back in the area heading the Fridays only Hope Street to Penmaenmawr working with 37685 on May 5th. **Photo Dave Trains.**

Above
50044 "Exeter" on the tail end of the Virgin "Pretendolino" stock near Glan Conwy on September 4th 2011. The train had worked down to Holyhead the day before, then on this day, worked to North Llanrwst prior to heading back to Euston. 57304 was leading the train at this point. This was the first visit of a class 50 to this part of the network since December 1992 when 50033 and 50050 made it all the way to Blaenau Ffestiniog on "The Festive Fifties" tour, see page 33.
Photo Peter Hanahoe.

Right
40145 heads 1Z51, "The Whistling Slater" railtour past Tal-y-Cafn en route to Blaenau Ffestiniog on June 4th 2005. Originating at Bristol Temple Meads, this service also visited Holyhead during the day. To date, this is the only occasion that 40145 has traversed this route in preservation but hopefully it will not be the last!
Photo Mark Lloyd Davies.

Left
The first, and to date, only pair of class 50s to traverse the Blaenau branch were 50050 and 50033 heading "The Festive Fifties" railtour on December 5th 1992. In this view they can be seen heading towards Blaenau Ffestiniog at Glan Dolwydellan. See also page 21.
Photo Dave Trains.

Below
The first class 50 to visit the Blaenau branch, 50018 heads the "Conway Crusader" railtour near Dolwyddelan on March 10th 1984. The return from Blaenau Ffestiniog would involve assistance from 40047.
Photo Peter Hanahoe.

Below
The use of class 37s on nuclear flask traffic to Trawsfynydd was very rare. However, on May 5th 1995, the failure of one of the class 31s booked for 7D38, the 06.40 Fridays only Llandudno Junction to Trawsfynydd duty resulted in 37107 being provided to team up with 31201 to cover the turn. In this view the pair are seen at Dolwydellan making their way down the Blaenau branch.
Photo Dave Trains.

Llandudno to Trawsfynydd

Right
The first visit of a class 37 to Blaenau Ffestiniog took place on May 3rd 1993 when 37422 worked 1D90, an 08.35 departure from Crewe to the town for naming "Robert F Fairlie". In this view it can be seen parked alongside a Fairlie locomotive operated by the Ffestiniog railway following the naming ceremony.
Photo Ken Robinson.

Left
The sight of a pair of Class Forties at Blaenau Ffestiniog was particularly unusual. However, on August 5th 1984, 40155 and 40015 were provided to work a BR Staff Association excursion from Stoke to the town. In this view they can be seen in the process of being run round the stock ready for the return journey.
Photo Ian Jordan.

Right
Following the success of the "Conway Crusader" tour to Blaenau Ffestiniog, see page 33, a repeat run was made a few weeks later on April 21st 1984. This time 50007 was used from Coventry before being paired up with 40192 for the round trip from Llandudno Junction to Blaenau. Here 1T12, the "Conway Crusader 2" is seen preparing to travel back up the branch to Llandudno Junction. On this occasion the train also visited Holyhead, 40086 taking over for that leg and on to Chester before handing over to 40122 and finally 40118!
Photo John Stephens.

Right
Following the closure of Trawsfynydd power station the last official flask train was worked by 31255 on August 8th 1995. However, on April 22nd 1997, one final flask was transported to the site and removed the following week. This was worked by 37426, recently overhauled and reliveried in EWS colours. In this view the locomotive is seen running around the train concerned at Blaenau Ffestiniog to propel it the six miles or so down to the power station.
Photo Ken Robinson.

Left
During 1989, six class 20s were converted by Hunslet Barclay Kilmarnock for use as privately owned locomotives on Schering/ Chipman's weed-killing trains. Numbered 20901 to 20906 they worked throughout the network. The first visit to North Wales came in September 1989 when 20902 and 20906 broke new ground for the class by working the weed-killer to Trawsfynydd and later to Amlwch. In this view, taken twelve months later on September 5th 1990, 20902(20060) and 20905 (20225) are seen passing the goods shed at Maentwrog Road on such a duty on their way back from Trawsfynydd to Llandudno Junction and on to Holyhead. All six locomotives would eventually be sold to DRS in August 1998. Of note is the use of 20902 on the "Kosovo Train for Life" with 20901 across Europe to Pristina in September 1999 where they were put to work for the United Nations for several months before a return to the UK via Macedonia.
Photo Peter Hanahoe.

Right
From May 1992, Trip 47 from Llandudno Junction was diagrammed for a class 40. This brought them to the section of line between Blaenau Ffestiniog and Trawsfynydd for the first time and were often seen working nuclear flask traffic from the power station at the end of the line up to Llandudno Junction for onward movement to Sellafield.
In this view, 40160 is seen on such a duty passing the disused Maentwrog Road station on February 16th 1984.
Photo Richard Thomas.

4.
Llandudno Junction to Bangor

Leaving Llandudno Junction the line passes the branch for Llandudno to the right before heading through Stephenson's first tubular bridge opened in April 1848. It then curves right and left through Conwy and along Conwy Morfa before reaching the 718 yard Penmaenbach tunnel. An open stretch between the sea and steeply rising hills follows, running alongside the sea past Dwygyfylchi. Penmaenmawr station and the quarry sidings on the right come next. English Electric traction, classes 20, 37 and 40 featured strongly here on various workings conveying quarried ballast to locations throughout the North West. On through Pen-y-Clip tunnel, into Llanfairfechan then along low ground through Aber. The line then crosses Ogwen viaduct over the Afon Ogwen before passing through the 506 yard Llandegai tunnel and past the site of Penrhyn sidings which had served Port Penrhyn via a short branch line until the early 1960's. Finally there is the 913 yard long Bangor tunnel prior to entering Bangor station which is situated between Bangor and Belmont tunnels with two through roads. The final class 40 hauled passenger service in North Wales during normal service for the class left Bangor behind 40152 on January 17th 1985 as 1E93 the 17.30 Bangor to York following the failure of the booked class 47. This was terminated at Chester due to the inability of 40152 to heat the train but I can imagine this issue would not have proved inconvenient for any enthusiast lucky enough to have been onboard! The remains of the goods yard situated on the left continued to be used for Engineers, Trip and Speedlink workings for several years during the period covered by this volume although this had closed by 1994 with the transfer of the tunnel inspection train that was based there, to Edge Hill.

Above
No doubting this is 40181! It looks to have a turbocharger problem as it speeds west with the 4D59 Manchester Trafford Park to Holyhead Freightliner in glorious evening sun on the 31st July 1984 at Tai'r Meibion farm crossing between Aber and Bangor. Up until the 1950s, there was a small signal box near here named after Tai'r Meibion farm which was a section splitter between here and Penrhyn sidings. One of the final class 40s to be withdrawn on January 21st 1985, 40181 was eventually cut up at Crewe works in October 1986.
Photo Peter Hanahoe.

Above
Following a number of years hard work by The Class Forty Preservation Society, "a Whistler" finally returned to the mainline when preserved 40145 worked "The Christmas Cracker" railtour from Crewe to Holyhead via Birmingham New Street and Manchester on November 30th 2002. Here it is seen pausing at Llandudno Junction en route Holyhead.
Photo Steve Morris.

Right
A smart looking 97408, ex 40118, is seen resting inside Llandudno Junction depot on July 23rd 1985, two months after being re-instated to traffic for departmental use. This was during a period of a few days when it strayed onto "normal" duties by working 4D11, the 22.41 Crewe to Bangor parcels on July 22nd followed by a special working to Derby conveying cripple wagons, just after this image was recorded.
Photo Ron Watson-Jones.

Above
January 17th 1985 and 40086 is seen shunting at Llandudno Junction yard during the last week of regular use for the class. A few weeks earlier on January 4th it had worked "the last" class 40 hauled passenger service out of Holyhead, an 01.25 relief to Birmingham. **Photo Ron Watson-Jones.**

Below
Taken from 37402, 37418 is seen at Conwy working 1K67, the 13.22 Bangor to Crewe on May 21st 1997.
Sold into preservation at the end of 2007, 37418 is currently based on the East Lancashire Railway.
Photo T Driver.

Above
By 1984, class 40 hauled passenger services were particularly rare. However, on May 31st, 40155 was provided for 1L70, a 17.20 Holyhead to Crewe additional service, pictured here at Conwy Morfa.
Photo Peter Hanahoe.

Below
The final class 40 hauled container train in North Wales was worked by 40122 as late as November 5th 1985. Having worked to Bangor on the 01.10 Chester parcels it replaced 47409 on 4H59, the 05.25 Holyhead to Trafford Park, seen here at Conwy Morfa. **Photo Ron Watson-Jones.**

Above
The summer of 1985 saw the introduction of class 20s to ballast duties out of Penmaenmawr. The first such working fell to 20049 and 20056, seen here heading along the sea wall at Penmaenmawr heading for St Helens on July 22nd.
Photo Ron Watson-Jones.

Below
A rare appearance of a double headed class 40 as late as July 25th 1985. Departmental examples 97405 (40060) and 97407 (40012) are seen approaching Penmaenmawr on 9X41, a train of track panels from Crewe bound for Valley.
Photo Ron Watson-Jones.

Above
June 1996 and 37888 is seen passing Dwygyfylchi near Penmaenmawr on 6E36, the empty RTZ coke hoppers to Immingham. **Photo Peter Hanahoe.**

Below
Sporting a new coat of DB Schenker livery, 37670 leads 37401 on a Holyhead to Carlisle excursion past Dwygyfylchi on August 2nd 2009. **Photo Peter Hanahoe.**

Above
With Penmaenbach Tunnel in the background, 37408 is seen running alongside the A55 "Expressway" on the approach to Penmaenmawr heading a Birmingham New Street to Holyhead service in June 1996.
Photo Peter Hanahoe.

Below
An unusual working for 37401. Having been sent light engine from Warrington to collect a wagon from Penmaenmawr that had spent a considerable time there waiting repair, the pair are seen heading back east near Penmaenmawr. April 28th 2009.
Photo Garnedd Jones.

Above
A classic view of 97407 (40012) "Aureol" during loading of a Wigan bound ballast train at Penmaenmawr on August 13th 1985. During the next two years the track layout in this area would be altered significantly as part of the A55 upgrade.
Photo Ron Watson-Jones.

Below
The second week of class 20 operation out of Penmaenmawr and 20194 partners 20196 on a St Helens bound ballast working. During this period, two trains were despatched to this location per day on Monday to Friday.
Photo Ron Watson-Jones.

Above
The first run of the Fridays only Manchester Hope Street to Penmaenmawr roadstone service ran on March 20th 1987 behind 37209 and 37129. In this view, the empties comprising 21 PHA bogie wagons are seen arriving at Penmaenmawr.
Photo Ron Watson-Jones.

Below
During the last part of 1987, 40122 was used on several local freight turns in North Wales. Having worked to Penmaenmawr on 7D30 ballast empties from Crewe it is seen here waiting to return as 7K11 on November 12th of that year.
Photo Ron-Watson Jones.

Above
An immaculate 37408 "Loch Rannoch" is seen waiting to depart Penmaenmawr on 6H19, a 16.15 service for Guide Bridge. The date is March 23rd 1994 and the appearance of an ETH 37 on such a duty was indeed unusual.
Photo Dave Trains.

Below
Even more surprising than the above was the use of EPS 37612 on the 6F36 13.05 Penmaenmawr to Edge Hill duty on February 20th 1996. Originally destined for the ill fated "Nightstar" services, sale to DRS followed in July 1997.
Photo Dave Trains.

Above
Having worked throughout to Holyhead on 1M86, the 13.00 from Cardiff the day before, 40122 was turned out for 1A56, the 12.45 to Euston on August 1st 1987. Here it is seen skirting the coast at Llanfairfechan heading for Crewe.
Photo Dave Trains.

Below
About to enter Pen-y-Clip tunnel near Llanfairfechan, 37420 heads 1K63, the 11.22 Bangor to Crewe on July 19th 1997. Withdrawn six months before the end of class 37 passenger duties in North Wales, final disposal took place at Hulls of Rotherham in February 2008. **Photo Dave Trains.**

Above
A shortage of 37/4s led to the use of Motherwell based 37403 "Ben Cruachan" in North Wales for several weeks during July 1999. In this view it is seen near Llanfairfechan working 1D77, the 16.21 Crewe to Bangor on the 12th of that month. The repaint into green livery had taken place at Glasgow works in February 1994 and remained until "403" was withdrawn in March 2000. **Photo Dave Trains.**

Below
During a two day period covering September 3rd and 4th 2011, 50044 top and tail with 57304, worked a charter from Euston to Holyhead and back with a "diversion" to Llanwrst North on the return journey. Interestingly, the spare Virgin West Coast MK3 set was used. In this view the service is seen at Llanfairfechan heading back to London on day two. **Photo Dave Trains.**

Above
April 29th 1984 and 40195 is seen engaged in Permanent Way work at Pentre Du crossing near Aber. Withdrawn from service two months later, final cutting would not come until the end of 1988 when it was attended to by A Hampton Ltd at Crewe works.
Photo Peter Hanahoe.

Below
With just over two weeks left in traffic, 40091 heads east near Aber with 3A19, the empty newspaper vans from Bangor. It is August 13th 1984, withdrawal would come on September 2nd. 40091 was the final class 40 to be cut up, the cabs not being dealt with until as late as February 1989.
Photo Peter Hanahoe.

Above
Named "Blackpool Tower" at Euston station on February 20th 1995, 37407 speeds past the site of the former Aber up distant signal on an evening Crewe to Bangor working during June of the same year. Withdrawn in March 2000, it would end up in preservation on the Churnet Valley Railway.
Photo Peter Hanahoe.

Below
DRS took over nuclear flask workings in North Wales at the end of 1998 with class 20's being the initial motive power chosen. Class 37's began to appear in mid 1999 and combinations of both types were then quite common. Here, 20302 and 37069 head a Valley to Sellafield working near Aber on July 28th 2009. **Photo Peter Hanahoe.**

Above
From October 2005, a weekly train of Cargowagons was operated from RTZ near Holyhead conveying aluminium billet for a customer in Ranshofen Austria. Class 37s worked this service on 45 occasions, sometimes double headed. A pair was turned out for the final train which ran on October 31st 2009. Here, the locomotives concerned, 37425 and 37401, can be seen near Aber heading the nine laden bogie vans to Warrington. **Photo Peter Hanahoe.**

Below
The final class 08 to leave Holyhead by rail was 08585. 37154 was used to move 08695 from Crewe to the port on June 6th 1993, returning with 08585 as 8P53 the day after. In this view, Llandudno Junction driver Dave Orford is seen at Tal-y-Bont with the return working on June 7th 1993. 08695 would be the last shunting locomotive to leave Holyhead, this time by road, from the flask loading sidings at Valley on January 11th 1995. **Photo Dave Trains.**

Above
Failure of the booked class 47 led to class 37s working London Euston bound MK3 rakes across the North Wales coast on a number of occasions during the 1990s and beyond, even assisting HST sets several times.
One of the most significant of these occurred on July 18th 1998 when 37131 was provided for the 1A37 08.50 Holyhead to Euston, seen here nearing Tal-y-Bont with a DVT/MK3 rake. Another non ETH example, 37212, repeated this working on the 17th of the following month, having also worked from Crewe to Holyhead the previous evening on the 17.10 from Euston.
Photo Dave Trains.

Below
On the day of the Britannia Bridge 150th anniversary celebrations, an Irish Mail headboard was carried by 37426 from Chester on the 10.07 Birmingham New Street to Holyhead. In this view, driver Ewan Williams is seen working the train through Aber on March 18th 2000.
Photo Peter Hanahoe.

Above
With some early morning mist still lingering, 37408 powers through Tal-y-Bont heading 1K59, the 09.13 Bangor to Crewe on December 27th 1995. A regular performer in North Wales, "Loch Rannoch" would end its days working Cardiff to Rhymney diagrams until a collision with stock at Rhymney on August 1st 2005 resulted in withdrawal. The end came at EMR Kingsbury in January 2008.
Photo Dave Trains.

Below
The last official day of class 37 locomotive haulage in North Wales was on Saturday December 30th 2000. 37429 had worked the first such service out of Holyhead back on May 17th 1993 as 1G80, the 03.20 for Birmingham International. It was therefore fitting that the same locomotive be entrusted to the final workings, two return trips Holyhead to Birmingham before a final run back to Crewe. In this view, Dave Trains is seen approaching Aber on 1D71, the 12.07 Birmingham New Street to Holyhead which he worked from Chester before handing over to Holyhead driver Bob Higgins for 1K73, the 15.58 to Crewe, and the end of an era.
Photo Peter Hanahoe.

Right

Class 37 hauled container trains in North Wales were not common. Apart from two surprise appearances in 1983, see volume 1, no others were recorded until September 2nd 1987 when 37204 and 37254 were sent light to Holyhead to work an 00.30 special to Stockton on Tees. What thought to be the final working for the class came on Saturday January 5th 1991 with 37706 turned out to work 4D53, the 12.37 departure from Crewe Basford Hall. Here it is seen approaching Llandegai Tunnel near Bangor. Container services in North Wales ceased just over two months later with closure of the Holyhead terminal on March 18th 1991.
Photo Dave Trains.

Below

Having covered the Amlwch to Llandudno Junction working earlier that day, see page 59, 40122 performed an unusual duty, seen here near Bangor heading for Holyhead with a single MK11 coach from Llandudno Junction. It then ran light to Valley to collect the nuclear flask train and returned to "The Junction" with this. A busy day! August 8th 1984.
Photo Peter Hanahoe.

Llandudno Junction to Bangor

Above
In common with class 37s, class 20 hauled container trains were also rare in North Wales. However, a failure at Chester on Saturday July 9th 1988 resulted in 20007 and 20053 being used on 4D52, the 07.12 departure from Basford Hall. Here they are seen bursting out of Llandegai tunnel near Bangor heading for Holyhead. **Photo Peter Hanahoe.**

Below
Other than running-in turns, the first class 37 hauled passenger service out of Holyhead ran on 13th August 1990 when 37430 was provided for a 1R58 14.15 relief to Euston. The first into Holyhead was 37427 on a Rugby special from Cardiff in March 1988 but this ran back ECS. Here the train is seen on the outskirts of Bangor. **Photo Dave Trains.**

Above
Another early class 37 passenger working took place on Sunday 23rd September 1990 when 37045 was used on a rake of air conditioned MK11's on 1D58, the 08.50 from Euston and 1A65, the 15.35 return between Crewe and Holyhead. In this view it is seen on the down working leaving Llandegai tunnel "wrong road" during engineering works. **Photo Dave Trains.**

Below
The final class 40 hauled container train to depart Holyhead ran on June 10th 1985 when 40122 worked 4K59, the 17.05 departure for Basford Hall. Here it is seen exiting Bangor Tunnel. See page 39 for details of the last class 40 hauled service of this type in North Wales, worked by 40122 from Bangor. **Photo Peter Hanahoe.**

Left
The final approach to Bangor station, about to exit Bangor tunnel. Loadhaul liveried is 37698 is seen waiting to depart on 1K65, the 12.22 to Crewe on June 5th 1999. This was during a two day period in North Wales when it was deputising for a 37/4.
Photo T Driver.

Below
April 1st 1984 and 40195 is seen at Bangor station waiting access to a worksite with an on-track crane during Sunday engineering duties.
Photo Steve Morris.

Right
Following the failure of 47638 "County of Kent" at Holyhead, 20140 and 20154 were despatched to tow it back to Crewe diesel depot. Here they are seen passing through Bangor as 9R00, a 16.45 departure from Holyhead during March 21st 1989.
20140 was scrapped by M.C Metal Processing in Glasgow in May 1994 but 20154 lives on in preservation on the GC Railway Nottingham. 47638 would eventually become 47845 prior to being rebuilt as 57301 which is currently in service with Network Rail. **Photo Dave Trains.**

Above
Other than on running-in turns, 37428 "David Lloyd George" was probably only the 3rd 37/4 to make it as far west as Bangor and an unusual choice for the 6L31 ballast trip working from Crewe on July 25th 1989. Here it can be seen shunting alongside Bangor station. **Photo Dave Trains.**

Below
The first 37/4 to be allocated to Cardiff Canton in February 1986, 37426 took up North Wales coast duties in December 1995 for a period of five years. In this view it can be seen waiting to depart Bangor on 2D71, the 20.22 service for Crewe on January 27th 1998. **Photo Dave Trains.**

5.
Bangor to Holyhead

On departing Bangor the line immediately enters the 648 yard Belmont tunnel before winding its way alongside the Menai Strait with views of Telford's suspension bridge to the right. Then it is onto Stephenson's Britannia Bridge linking the mainland to Anglesey, a tubular structure as at Conwy but this time 504 yards long and over 100 feet above water level. A huge fire which started on May 23rd 1970 resulted in the closure of the bridge so severing the rail link to Anglesey until reopening in a modified form, minus the tubes, on January 30th 1972. A road deck was then added, opening in July 1980.

On leaving the bridge the line curves to the left and on through Llanfair PG. Next comes Gaerwen with the branch to Amlwch off to the right which remained open for freight traffic to Associated Octel until 1994 although the only "EE" traction to appear on these services would be the class 40. West of Gaerwen the line descends the 1 in 97/102 Llangaffo Bank to sea-level and Malltraeth marsh. Over Bodorgan viaduct then a 1 in 98 climb through two tunnels on the approach to Bodorgan station before heading through Ty Croes and Rhosneigr, with views of RAF Valley on the left. Then through Valley, with sidings to the right for general use and from the early 1970s onwards, a loading point for nuclear flasks from the nearby Wylfa power station. From 1989 the introduction of a triangle here provided a turning point for steam locomotives used on numerous special working along the North Wales coast. The nuclear flask services were, and remain, a bastion for English Electric traction, classes 20, 37 and 40 being regular performers, the former two still seeing use today! The line then runs onto the Stanley, a causeway linking Anglesey with Holy Island before passing the RTZ Anglesey Aluminium smelter, opened in 1970 and served by numerous class 40 class 37 hauled flows including inbound petroleum coke and outbound finished product right up until closure in 2009. A drop down a 1 in 135 gradient past Ty Mawr farm on the left and past the disused water tower on the right follows before the line runs under what was locally known as "Canada Gardens" bridge to pass between Holyhead depot on the right and the former cattle/goods yard on the left which was removed as part of the A55 Expressway project in 1999. We then reach the end of the line at Holyhead station, just over 84 miles from Chester.

Above
Saturday 30th December 2000, the "final" day of class 37 locomotive hauled services in North Wales. Driver Dave Trains takes a few seconds to record 37429 on 1D71, the 12.07 Birmingham New Street to Holyhead on arrival at Bangor at 15.16 before climbing back in and heading off to Holyhead for one last time. Finally, 37415 and 37429 would work Holyhead to Birmingham diagrams as late as January 19th and 20th respectively due to the late entry to service of new 175108, but then it was over.

Above
The first class 20 hauled passenger working west of Bangor took place on October 26th 1988 when 20158 and 20139 rescued failed 47611 on 1D33, the 07.55 from Coventry. Here they can be seen heading for Holyhead departing Bangor 76 minutes late. **Photo Dave Trains.**

Below
40122 passes Menai Bridge yard at the head of 7D05, the morning Amlwch to Llandudno Junction freight. The consist comprises a mixture of ethylene dibromide and liquid chlorine tankers along with several empty sulphur hoppers. August 8th 1984. **Photo Peter Hanahoe.**

Above
Sulphur, imported into Mostyn docks was conveyed to the Associated Octel plant at Amlwch in vacuum braked HJV/ HKV wagons. One such working is seen behind 40104 at Menai Bridge on June 13th 1984. The final train of this type would run on May 17th 1989. **Photo Peter Hanahoe.**

Below
August 1993 and 37421 takes the single line at Treborth to cross Britannia Bridge hauling a Birmingham New Street to Holyhead service. This image was taken from the closed Caernarfon branch alignment, the track having been removed over twenty years earlier. **Photo Peter Hanahoe.**

Above
Class 20 hauled container trains were rarely seen in North Wales so no apologies for another view of 20007 and 20053, see also page 54, on 4D52, the 07.12 departure from Basford Hall which they worked from Chester before returning light engine. Here they are seen passing Llanfair PG signal box heading for Holyhead.
Other class 20 hauled "Liners" recorded at Holyhead were 20005 and 20135 on December 5th 1986, the first working for the class to the port of any kind, 20078 and 20082 arriving light to work an 02.20 departure on April 16th 1988, and 20020 with 20021 working in and out on such a duty during October 24th 1989.
Photo Dave Trains.

Right
Overlooked by The Marquis of Anglesey, 37422 powers through Llanfair PG on a Birmingham to Holyhead working during September 1993. Following six years passenger work in North Wales, 37422 was given a light overhaul at Cardiff Canton following over three years in store and named "Cardiff Canton", the plates having previously been carried by 56044. Further passenger work between Cardiff and Rhymney followed for several years before more general use by EWS until withdrawal in September 2008. Following several years languishing at Toton depot, 37422 was sold to DRS along with several other 37/4's for possible refurbishment and further use. At the time of writing it is undergoing overhaul by DRS at Carlisle Kingmoor depot.
Photo Peter Hanahoe.

Above
Dawn on September 16th 2003 and 37029 and 37038 are near Llanfair PG working 7D41, the 05.38 Crewe to Valley empty flasks. At the time of writing, 37038 remains active with DRS although 37029 has now entered preservation and is currently located at the Epping Ongar railway.
Photo T Driver.

Below
Gaerwen, Sunday 9th March 1997. 37370 passes on 7L34, a 14.30 ballast to Bangor. Fitted with re geared CP7 bogies and renumbered from 37127 in July 1988, a main generator flashover in November 2000 spelt the end for 37370 with cutting coming at Booths Rotherham in September 2005.
Photo Dave Trains.

Above
With driver John Humphries in charge, 20309 and 20303 pass Llangaffo summit working a Fathers Day Crewe to Holyhead Northern Belle on June 19th 2011. 47818 was on the rear of the train and the return was triple headed as far as Rhyl where the failure of 20303 resulted in the class 47 working on alone.
Photo Peter Hanahoe.

Below
A perfect summer's day in August 1993 sees 37414 heading along the embankment west of Malltraeth viaduct on a Birmingham New Street to Holyhead service.
Photo Peter Hanahoe.

Above

37430 "Cwmbran" heads a scratch set of stock ECS to Holyhead to work a relief to the afternoon boat train, seen here between Maltraeth viaduct and Bodorgan tunnels. The date is August 13th 1990 and other than running-in turns, the resulting 1R58 14.15 departure would be the first class 37 hauled passenger service out of Holyhead. See also page 54.
Photo Peter Hanahoe.

Left

Taken from 37414, 37421 approaches the 413 yard Bodorgan No2 tunnel on 1G97, the 10.48 Holyhead to Birmingham New Street on June 16th 1998. Just prior to this, No1 tunnel is the shorter of the two at 115 yards.
Photo T Driver.

Above
Showing an incorrect headcode, 55016 nears Ty Croes heading for Holyhead on 1Z41, a charter from Milton Keynes which it worked from Chester and all the way back to Buckinghamshire as 1Z42. September 7th 2002. **Photo Dave Trains.**

Below
Anglesey is not as flat as you might think! During a rare visit to North Wales, 37430 is seen between Ty Croes and Bodorgan heading a Holyhead to Birmingham New Street service during July 1996. **Photo Peter Hanahoe.**

Above
A regular double headed working took place on a Sunday during the class 37 loco hauled diagrams in North Wales. During 2000 this involved 1D60, the 15.41 Crewe to Holyhead and 1G79, the 18.27 Holyhead to Birmingham International. In this view taken on May 14th 2000, 37426 leads 37429 on the down working at Llanfaelog near Rhosneigr. **Photo Peter Hanahoe.**

Below
DRS currently operates Railhead Treatment Train (RHTT) duties in North Wales. Since introduction of the FEA container flat and "module" concept in 2005, these services have either been top and tailed or covered single handed, mainly by class 37's. During 2008, the circuit including Anglesey was covered by a single class 37. In this view, 37423 is seen near Rhosneigr on the return working to Crewe on November 20th. **Photo Steve Morris.**

Above
A pair of DRS class 20s are seen on the approach to Rhosneigr station heading the afternoon Valley to Crewe nuclear flask working during February 2003. In later years the use of barrier wagons would cease.
Photo Peter Hanahoe.

Left
During 2011 the RHTT diagram in North and mid Wales was covered by two of Network Rail's ERTMS fitted class 37's. In this view 97304 (37217) and 97302 (37170) are seen near Rhosneigr working towards Holyhead on October 7th at the start of the leaf-fall season.
Photo Garnedd Jones.

Above
37412 heads past the outskirts of Rhosneigr on a Sunday afternoon service for Crewe on September 5th 1999. A late arrival on the North Wales scene, it had been allocated to Crewe two months prior to this working and would remain there until late 2000 prior to taking up Rhymney valley duties.
Photo Steve Morris.

Below
Mixed pair 20303 and 37688 near Rhosneigr on March 28th 2011 heading for Crewe on the return flask working from Valley. By now anything from the DRS fleet could turn up on this service, including pairs of class 57s and 66s!
Photo Mark Lloyd Davies.

Above
RAF Valley, November 22nd 1997. With Snowdonia in the background 37420 is seen on the last leg of its journey on the 1D57, Saturdays only 05.06 Birmingham New Street to Holyhead. Withdrawn as early as July 2000, 37420 was cut up at Hull's Rotherham in February 2008.
Photo T Driver.

Below
The "Holy Oakes" charter run by Spitfire railtours ran from Weston-super-Mare to Holyhead on March 26th 2011. Worked top and tail by 37685/37676 and 57601 this was, at the time of writing, the last class 37 hauled passenger working to visit Holyhead. Here the return service is seen passing RAF Valley. **Photo Mark Lloyd Davies.**

Bangor to Holyhead

Above
During a five week period in 1992, a short term flow of scrap from the RTZ Aluminium smelter near Holyhead to Allied Steel and Wire Cardiff was operated. 37902/903/904 all featured along with 37710 and in the above case, the only double headed working with 37213 and 37717, seen here with the Mondays only 6Z26 17.30 departure near Caergeiliog on April 13th. **Photo Peter Hanahoe.**

Below
As mentioned earlier, a variety of motive power can turn up on the DRS flask workings to and from Valley. In this case it is a class 20/57 combination. 20309 and 57008 are seen at the same location as the above image heading for Crewe on June 15th 2011. The signal they are passing is an emergency signal for the nearby RAF Valley and rarely if ever used. **Photo Garnedd Jones.**

Above
37401 powers out of Valley on the weekly Cargowagon working between RTZ and Warrington. The date is August 1st 2009 and this was the first appearance of a class 37 on this service, 37401 having worked in with the empties and back light a few days earlier. See page 50 for the final working of this interesting flow. **Photo Garnedd Jones.**

Below
The use of non ETH fitted class 37s on North Wales passenger duties during the summer months was quite common. 37069 enjoyed a ten day spell helping out between May 31st and June 9th 1998. Here it is seen just outside Valley on 1G11, the 13.54 Holyhead to Birmingham on June 1st. **Photo Dave Trains.**

Above
A view of Valley triangle being put to good use with 37087 and 37608 running round their flask train on May 28th 2009. In June 2012, 37087 was one of the first of the DRS operational 37s to be withdrawn. **Photo Garnedd Jones.**

Below
August 2nd 2009. 37670 plus 37401 head a Compass Tours charter from Holyhead to Carlisle through Valley. Having been given a coat of DB Schenker livery a few weeks before, 37670 would be withdrawn on September 4th! **Photo Garnedd Jones.**

Above
Right up to date, August 21st 2012 and class 20s are getting rarer on flask duties. Here, with approaching 100 years service between them, 20308 (20187) and 20305 (20095) depart Valley for Crewe. **Photo Garnedd Jones.**

Below
The first class 37 hauled flask working took place under Trainload Freight on May 10th 1994. Here, the working in question, 7C40 , the 14.12 Tuesdays only to Sellafield is seen behind 37675 at the loading point in Valley. **Photo T Driver.**

Above
40145 makes a fine sight storming through Valley on the Compass Tours "Pennine Fellsman" charter to Durham on May 25th 2009. With load 12 plus 47815 on the back this was a good test for the 40, one which it passed with flying colours! **Photo Peter Hanahoe.**

Below
May 13th 1984 and 40174 is seen on the approach to Valley working an up relief. A "London Midland" locomotive throughout its career, 40174 was withdrawn ten days after this image was recorded following just over 22 years service. **Photo Peter Hanahoe.**

Above
37069 passes over The Cob linking Holy Island to Anglesey on a return RHTT working during November 2008. This particular example spent over 12 months working in France for EWS prior to being purchased by DRS in September 2001. **Photo Mark Lloyd Davies.**

Below
Immingham based 37699 waits to depart RTZ Anglesey Aluminium with the coke empties to the Humber Conoco refinery on April 17th 1994. A fleet of 17 PAB wagons was dedicated to this traffic between 1971 and 2001 until a fire closed part of the refinery. **Photo Pat Webb.**

Above
40181 is seen engaged in tack renewal work alongside the RTZ works on the outskirts of Holyhead on Saturday July 28th 1984. The following day it would work the coke empties out of the plant.
Photo Steve Morris.

Below
The daily Llandudno Junction Trip 30 approaches Holyhead on April 3rd 1984 behind 40195. The previous year on September 2nd 1983, the only class 40 hauled rake of MK3 coaches had been worked into Holyhead by this example.
Photo Steve Morris.

Above
A bad day for the 37/4s! Motherwell based 37175 departs Holyhead on 1G86, the 16.50 to Birmingham New Street, taken from another interloper, 37069 working into the town from the same location. June 8th 1998.
Photo T Driver.

Below
37422 climbs the 1 in 135 gradient out of Holyhead at the head of the 14.22 service to Crewe on September 17th 1995. A mixture of MK1 and MK11 coaches follow, the full train in Regional Railways livery.
Photo Steve Morris.

Left
37800 partners 33057 on 1V09, the 14.08 Holyhead to Cardiff out of Holyhead on August 27th 1986. This was during a period between October 1985 and May 1987 when refurbished class 37s undertook running-in turns on Cardiff to Bangor or Holyhead services from and back to Crewe, along with the booked class 33 or 47. The final such working is thought to have involved 37678 and 47603 on 1D27, the 11.17 from Crewe and 1V09 return on May 6th 1987 prior to the diagram going over to Sprinter operation.
Photo Garnedd Jones.

Right
October 8th 1999 and failed 50017 is seen on the tail of a return charter to Euston leaving Holyhead headed by 55019. This was the first time a Deltic had visited the town and first sighting of a class 50 for almost 7 years. 55019 had been added to the train at Crewe due to the failure of the 50 earlier in the day. The livery carried by 50017 was applied during a period of use with VSOE at Crewe where it was based for working trains such as this. This was short lived, the duties being taken over by EWS. It now resides at the Plym Valley Railway having recently been overhauled and repainted in Network SouthEast livery.
Photo Andy Morris.

Left
DRS provide motive power to DB Schenker infrastructure monitoring based in Derby to work track monitoring trains for Network Rail. These often use class 37s in top and tail mode. In this view, 37605 and 37603 are seen leaving Holyhead heading a measurement train back to Derby on May 17th 2012. Originally refurbished as 37507 and 37504 respectively, they were renumbered when converted for use by European Passenger Services in 1995. Both were sold to DRS in 2002 following the cancellation of the "Nightstar" services that they were intended to work.
Photo Mark Lloyd Davies.

6.
Amlwch branch

Leaving the mainline at Gaerwen, the branch to Amlwch was opened fully in 1867. During the period covered by this volume it was frequented by class 40s up until the end of 1984 on workings to and from the Associated Octel chemical plant at Amlwch. Trainloads of sulphur were transported there from Mostyn Dock up until 1989. In the other direction, consignments of chlorine and ethylene dybromide were despatched from Amlwch to Ellesmere Port and anti-knock compound to a number of UK and European refineries. Altogether this amounted to a total of approximately 70,000 tonnes per annum. No other English Electric locos worked the line regularly although a number of charter trains utilised classes 20 and 37 during the period in question. An early if not first class 20 visit was made by 20902/906 on a Hunslet Barclay weed-killer duty on September 22nd 1989. The branch was closed in 1994 following the transfer of the rail traffic to road and the facility at Amlwch itself closed in 2005. At the time of writing there is an initiative in place to re-open the line for passenger traffic as far as Llangefni although whether this comes to anything remains to be seen.

Above
As with volume 1 of this series, a number of railtours visited the Amlwch branch during the period covered by this volume, regular passenger services having ceased as early as 1964. One of these, the "Anglesey Odyssey 1" on September 11th 1993 featured top and tail class 20s and 37s working to Amlwch on September 11th 1993, the train having originated at Cardiff. In this view, 37225 and 37075 tail 20169 and 20118 through Tryfil near Llanerchymedd on the return working from Amlwch. 20169 carries the BR Technical Services Division livery having been allocated there five months previously. The second tour in the series, "The Anglesey Odyssey 2" ran from York four weeks later on October 9th and featured 37422 top and tail with 20138/20066 to Amlwch. The class 20's were replaced by 20075/187 at Crewe on the return run prior to visiting Silverdale colliery before 37422 worked the train back to York.
The final official freight to traverse the branch would run a few weeks following the above working on the 29th of September behind 47228 although a number of others ran as required up until February 10th 1994 when 31126 worked 6P05, an 08.55 Amlwch to Llandudno Junction, so bringing the use of the line to an end some 127 years after being fully opened.
Photo Dave Trains.

Amlwch branch

Above
40104 heads a well loaded 7D04, Llandudno Junction to Amlwch goods up the gradient through the woods from Cefni Reservoir towards Llangwyllog on June 11th 1984. Note the Royal Train headcode! **Photo Peter Hanahoe.**

Below
Another view of "The Anglesey Odyssey 1" tour, this time on the outbound leg with 37225/075 leading 20169/118 seen between Llangwyllog and Llanerchymedd. September 11th 1993. **Photo Peter Hanahoe.**

Above
October 9th 1993 and "The Anglesey Odyssey 2" railtour is seen returning from Amlwch behind 20066/138 near Llangwyllog. 37422 is on the rear.
Photo Peter Hanahoe.

Right
40135 heads 8L40, a sulphur working from Mostyn Docks to Amlwch near Llanerchymedd on May 2nd 1984. This traffic would cease by the end of May 1989.
Photo Dave Trains.

Left
What was probably the first visit of a class 20 to the Amlwch branch took place on September 22nd 1989. Here 20902 and 20906 top and tail 7Z07, a Hunslet Barclay weed-killer duty from Llandudno Junction to Amlwch past Rhosgoch. Later in the day it would also cover the line to Holyhead, the previous day it had travelled to Trawsfynydd, see page 35.
Photo Dave Trains.

Amlwch branch

Above
"The Mabinogion" railtour was run from Euston to Amlwch on October 16th 1993. 37218/261 were provided top and tail with 47513, the class 37's seen here on the return trip passing the disused Rhosgoch sidings. **Photo Darran Moss.**

Below
40122 passes Rhosgoch heading 7D05, the morning Amlwch to Llandudno Junction working on August 8th 1984. See also page 53 for another duty covered by 40122 on this particular day. **Photo Peter Hanahoe.**

Above
Working hard, the ghostly hulk of 40135 appears through the early morning mist near Llanerchymedd on 7D04, the Llandudno Junction to Amlwch goods on August 17th 1984. **Photo Peter Hanahoe.**

Below
September 11th 1984. 40013 has just arrived at the Associated Octel plant at Amlwch. It would now uncouple and stable in the spur on the left hand side to allow the local 0-4-0 shunter to take the train into the plant. **Photo Peter Hanahoe.**

7.
Holyhead

The end of the line! In contrast with volume 1 in this series, class 37s were the most regular "EE" product to make it as far as Holyhead during the period covered by volume 2. The class started regular association with the town on May 17th 1983 with the introduction of class 37 hauled passenger diagrams serving North Wales. They were also used in increasing numbers on freight workings to and from the port such as the occasional container train and other flows including fuel oil for Holyhead depot and services to and from RTZ Anglesey Aluminium.

The final class 40 working out of Holyhead prior to end of regular service for the class took place on January 6th 1985 with 40060 heading a special container service to York. 40086 had headed the final passenger working from the port two days earlier on 1G00, an 01.25 relief to Birmingham. There would of course be a number of other appearances for the class at Holyhead but these were limited to 40122 and more recently, preserved 40145. Some 53 years since the first appearance of a class 40 at Holyhead, other visits are very likely thanks to The Class Forty Preservation Society.

Class 20s first appeared on the scene on December 5th 1986 with 20005/135 heading a special container train to the port, something that would be repeated several times during the next few years. The class broke ground on a passenger working that far west on October 26th 1988 with 20158/139 towing a dead 47611 to its destination at the head of the 07.55 from Coventry. Class 20's never featured in any regular capacity on workings to Holyhead although they often turned up having rescued failures or on additional freight workings, making a nice change from the norm.

Class 50s had been reasonably frequent visitors during the mid 1970s on both passenger and Freightliner turns but during the period covered by this volume only three appearances would be recorded, all on charter services although in one case, see page 78, the locomotive concerned, 50017, was in fact "dead". Finally, something that could only have been dreamed of when the class was in regular service, "Deltics" have made three visits to Holyhead to date since entering preservation. The first involved the use of 55019 heading a charter from Coventry on October 8th 1999 following the failure of 50017 as mentioned above.

Above
June 5th 1997 and 37421 is seen refuelling on Holyhead shed at 3am. Refurbished in June 1985 from 37267, this example spent the first five years as a 37/4 working off Inverness during which time it spent a period isolated on the north side of the River Ness following the collapse of the Ness bridge on the outskirts of Inverness during flooding in February 1989.
Photo Dave Trains.

Holyhead

Right
On the run up to the final
withdrawal of 40122 a number
of farewell tours were operated.
It was only fitting that one of
these featured North Wales so
on April 2nd 1988 "The
Tubular Belle" ran to Blaenau
Ffestiniog, Llandudno and
Holyhead. In this view it can be
seen on the final approach to
Holyhead station. The final run
would take place two weeks
later between London
Liverpool Street, Norwich and
York prior to being handed
over to The National Railway
Museum. See page 94 for the
next class 40 to visit Holyhead.
Photo Pat Webb.

Left
Something that had been a
common sight for train crew
for many years, the view from
a class 40 attacking the 1 in 93
gradient out of Holyhead. In
this case it is from 40122
heading the "final" class 40
hauled passenger service out of
the town in tandem with 47427
on 1A78, the 16.15 to Euston.
The date is February 9th 1988
and it is likely that it had ended
up on this turn as a trial run
following attention at Crewe
diesel depot having worked in
on 1D43 the 09.30 from
Euston earlier in the day.
Photo Garnedd Jones.

Right
Class 50s often visited
Holyhead under the cover of
darkness during the mid 1970s,
a regular diagram being the
19.15 from Euston and 00.55
return which they worked from
and to Crewe. However, apart
running-in turns to Bangor that
were reported to have featured
a pair on at least one occasion,
double headers were unknown.
In this image, the only double
headed 50 to reach Holyhead to
date is seen waiting to depart
behind 50033 and 50050 at the
head of "The Festive Fifties"
railtour back to Euston on
December 5th 1992. See also
pages 21 and 33.
Photo Pat Webb.

Left
July 9th 1988. 20007 and 20053 enter Holyhead Freightliner terminal at the head of 4D52, the 07.12 departure from Crewe Basford Hall. One of the first appearances for the class as far west as Holyhead, they had replaced a failed class 47 at Chester. See also page 61.
Photo Pat Webb.

Below
Another class 20 hauled container train, 4K59, the 17.56 to Basford Hall waits to depart Holyhead behind 20021/020 on October 24th 1989.
Photo Garnedd Jones.

Left
The first class 37 hauled "Liner" to Holyhead was as early as April 1983 when 37165 turned up on an additional working from Felixstowe, something that was repeated by 37173 a few weeks later, see volume 1. However, the class remained extremely rare on such duties with only a handful of others being recorded prior to closure of the Holyhead terminal on March 18th 1991.
In this view, Stratford based 37888 waits to depart Holyhead on the 06.40 Basford Hall working on March 10th 1988. Only one other class 37 would appear on such a duty, see page 53.
Photo Garnedd Jones.

Above
Even before the removal of the facing crossover into the plant, coke workings into RTZ Anglesey Aluminium regularly ran through to Holyhead to run around to permit them to propel the load into the plant. In this view, 37676 waits to be uncoupled having just arrived on platform 1 Holyhead station on 6M43, the 18.00 Tuesdays only Humber refinery to Holyhead RTZ. November 5th 1997. **Photo Dave Trains.**

Below
37408 "Loch Rannoch" enters Holyhead on a working from Crewe on April 6th 1996. One of the first eight members of the class to be allocated to North Wales coast duties in May 1993, it would remain in the area until a move to Motherwell in April 2000.
Photo Steve Morris.

Holyhead

Above & below
November 1984. By now the sight of a class 40 stabled on Holyhead shed was rare, the majority of remaining workings being off Llandudno Junction. However, over the weekend of the 17th and 18th of November, two examples found themselves parked up at Holyhead. 40181, above, would remain in traffic until the end of regular use for the class in January 1985. 40013, below, worked the Trafford Park Freightliner out of the town on Monday 19th November and would remain in traffic for a further seven weeks. It can currently be found undergoing restoration at Barrow Hill. 40181 was not so lucky!
Photos Steve Morris.

Above
What was probably the first visit of a class 37 to Holyhead shed took place on May 16th 1988. 37431 had been sent light engine from Crewe to tow failed 47340 away for repair but then failed itself on the shed due to a mistake that resulted in its firebottles being discharged. Here the two locomotives concerned await rescue from Holyhead shed. **Photo Pat Webb.**

Below
A rare sighting of class 20s on shed at Holyhead. 20902 and 20906 are seen with the Hunslet Barclay weed-killing train being serviced at the fuelling point having just arrived following a visit to Amlwch, see page 81.
September 22nd 1989.
Photo Garnedd Jones.

Above
The only 37/9 to visit Holyhead shed was 37903. Having arrived on the first ASW to RTZ scrap working on March 30th 1992 it needed fuel, hence the above image. This train would run a further four times, see also page 70.
Photo Garnedd Jones.

Below
The first class 40 to come onto Holyhead shed in over 17 years was preserved 40145. It needed servicing whilst working "The Whistling Slater" railtour on June 5th 2005, which also visited Blaenau Ffestiniog. See also page 32.
Photo Garnedd Jones.

Above
"John Bangor", John Williams, Brendon Murray, Cyril Blakeway, Tommy Caine, John Burton and "John Bach Bryngwran" pose alongside 08788 "Caergybi" on Holyhead shed.

Top left - John Humphreys with 20309 running round "The Northern Belle" at Holyhead on June 19th 2011.

Top right - Dave Trains & Mike Lunn with a 47/8 at Bangor. **Photo Barry Wynne.**

Left - Garnedd Jones and Eric Bailey Williams on 40122. Holyhead, August 1987.

Right - Glyn Williams and Henry Charlton with 40181. Valley, July 28th 1984.

Left - Jimmy Lawson alongside 40122. Holyhead shed. Summer 1987.

Bottom left - Jock Slavin and 37417 having worked the "Stanlow Tanks" into Holyhead on October 22nd 1994.

Bottom right - Tom Hughes and 20053. Holyhead Freightliner terminal. July 9th 1988.

Below - Charlie Gregory with 40122 on February 9th 1988 en route Holyhead shed after arriving at the port on the 09.30 from Euston.

All photos by Garnedd Jones unless otherwise stated.

North Wales Coast Railwaymen

Above
Another class 47 failure sees 37408 waiting to leave Holyhead on a MK3/DVT rake on 1A29, the 09.05 Euston service on March 3rd 1995.
Photo Pat Webb.

Left
The first DRS class 20s to visit Holyhead were 20302/301 on a trial run from Crewe prior to a Royal Train duty. Here they are on arrival, May 30th 1996. See also page 15.
Photo Garnedd Jones.

Right
The morning of August 5th 1998 and 37418 has come to grief at the entrance to Holyhead shed. 37426 departs the town for Crewe. The breakdown vans would finally arrive from Crewe behind 47572 at 17.30.
Photo Pat Webb.

Above
During May 1998, Regional Railways hired a class 37 from DRS on several occasions, the first being 37610 which rescued 37414 on the 16.50 Crewe to Holyhead on May 6th. 37611 also had a period working "The Coast" and is seen here entering Holyhead on 1D75, the 14.23 from Birmingham on May 21st 1998. **Photo Dave Trains.**

Below
A regular visitor to North Wales on freight duties, Toton based 37675 found itself deputising for a 37/4 on North Wales passenger turns for several days in June 1999. In this view it is waiting to depart Holyhead on 1K67, the 12.51 for Crewe on June 9th.
Photo Pat Webb.

Holyhead

Left
Porterbrook liveried 55016 departs Holyhead on 1Z42, a return charter to Milton Keynes on September 7th 2002.
Photo Mark Lloyd Davies.

Below
Following a number of years hard work by The Class Forty Preservation Society, 40145 returned to the mainline at the head of "The Christmas Cracker" tour on November 30th 2002. Here it is seen waiting to depart Holyhead on the return journey. To date, a further two visits have been made by 40145 to the town on railtour duty.
Photo Steve Morris.

Below
Non availability of the booked pair of class 33s resulted in 37689 and 37667 working the Pathfinder Tours "North Wales and Snowdonia" charter from Swindon to Holyhead on June 19th 2004. By this stage in their lives both examples were high on engine hours and allocated primarily to Sandite duties. Following overhaul, 37667 lives on in service with DRS. In this view they can be seen passing Holyhead shed on 1Z33 the inbound leg of the working.
Photo Ken Robinson.

Above
Following the reinstatement of 37423, 37409 became the second 37/4 to be returned to traffic by DRS in May 2010. One of its first duties was to work an inspection saloon to Holyhead, seen here entering the town on June 23rd 2010. **Photo Garnedd Jones.**

Below
Prior to the start of RHTT operation in 2011, three days of trial runs were undertaken using 20901 and 20905 hired in from Harry Needle Railroad company. In this view taken on the first day, 27th September 2011, they can be seen leaving Holyhead on the return to Crewe. **Photo Garnedd Jones.**

Holyhead

Above
Further to the RHTT trial runs mentioned on the previous page, the booked traction took over on September 30th 2011. 97302 (ex 37170) and 97304 (ex 37217) wait to depart Holyhead for Crewe at 10.48. The full working, began on October 3rd with the 97s covering the complete diagram. **Photo Garnedd Jones.**

Below
We end this volume with a view of 50044 "Exeter" operating top and tail with 57304 climbing out of Holyhead on a return charter to London Euston on September 4th 2011. A diversion to North Llanwrst would take place en route, see page 32. This was the first visit of an operational member of the class to Holyhead for over 18 years. **Photo Garnedd Jones.**